# SWANAGE AND PURBECK

## IN OLD PHOTOGRAPHS

SANDBANKS FERRY in the 1930s. The first steam ferry came into operation in 1926 but was withdrawn almost immediately with engine trouble and a defect in the prow-lifting gear. Once this was resolved the new ferry service soon became an essential link for Studland and Swanage, reducing the journey to Bournemouth from a round trip of twenty-five miles to only nine miles. The Hants and Dorset bus service from Bournemouth to Swanage was due to commence in May 1926, but owing to the problems with the ferry, mentioned above, and the effects of the General Strike the service (Route No. 12A) did not start until April 1927. It was renumbered No. 7 from 1940. *Floating Bridge* No. 3 was built by Bolson and Son of Poole in 1958 and replaced an earlier steam ferry.

Front Cover Illustration:
THE HIGH STREET, July 1902. The Town Hall was completed in 1882, with the addition of the front of Mercers' Hall from Cheapside, London. Designed by Edward Jerman, a pupil of Sir Christopher Wren, this imposing façade was one of the many acquisitions with which George Burt embellished his native town.

# SWANAGE AND PURBECK IN OLD PHOTOGRAPHS

COLLECTED BY
DAVID HAYSOM AND DAVID BRAGG

Alan Sutton Publishing Limited
Phoenix Mill · Far Thrupp · Stroud · Gloucestershire

First published 1991



**British Library Cataloguing in Publication Data**

Swanage and Purbeck in old photographs.
I. Haysom, David, *1957–*
II. Bragg, David, *1926–*
942.336

ISBN 0-86299-889-1

Typeset in 9/10 Korinna.
Typesetting and origination by
Alan Sutton Publishing Limited.
Printed in Great Britain by
The Bath Press, Avon.

# CONTENTS

# INTRODUCTION

The selection of photographs in this book show the changing face of Swanage, from the centre of the stone trade to the seaside resort we know today, and the influence of the railway is also recognized. Other sections include the Purbeck villages, people and events, the two world wars and the excellent work of the Swanage lifeboat and local fire brigade. Where known, the name of the photographer is quoted at the end of each caption.

The original photographs came principally from older local residents who kindly allowed new negatives to be made by John Rutherford, Swanage's local professional photographer since 1963. Naturally, we have included some of his photographs.

The earliest known resident photographer was Isaac French who ran a short-lived studio in the mid-1860s. The photographs from the next twenty years are the work of national photographic companies who produced souvenir views of the fashionable seaside resorts.

In 1888 the Dorchester-based photographer Walter Pouncy (1844–1918) opened a studio in the High Street at Swanage (near the Red Lion). His father, John Pouncy (1818–1894), had established a 'House Painting, Decorating and Glazing' business at Dorchester in 1845; but his interest soon turned to experimenting with photography. In 1857 he published *Dorsetshire Photographically Illustrated*, acknowledged as the *first* book in the world to contain photographs. Around 1860 Walter entered his father's business at 38 High West Street, Dorchester, which now included photography. By 1870 John Pouncy had opened a new studio at 9 South Street and Walter took over the original studio. The census of 1871 reveals that Walter was employing three men and a boy. Walter married in around 1882, and in 1884 their only child Florence was born.

Walter's new studio in Swanage opened in January 1888. He appointed a young man named Thomas Powell as manager. Powell was born in Herefordshire on 21 October 1860, and moved to Dorset around 1880, becoming an apprentice to John Pouncy in Dorchester. Here Thomas was to learn the art of photography from one of its earliest pioneers. Thomas married a Miss Samways from Warmwell, and on 16 March 1882 their first child William was born.

When Thomas Powell moved to Swanage his family lived above Pouncy's shop in the High Street. Many of his early photographs show scenes and local characters near the shop. Thomas made his own camera, one of the earliest hand-held types taking quarter plate glass negatives. The body was made of cigar box wood and the lens cost 4s. 6d. This camera was used to take a number of photographs in this book.

Powell also used a mobile photographic studio sited on Shore Road, which also advertised Pouncy's shop where visitors could purchase his 'Town and County Views'. In 1896 Pouncy had a new studio built in the High Street (named The Arcade), with large windows and a special skylight. Thomas Powell acted as manager until he set up his own studio in 1898, when Pouncy closed the new shop. It was taken over by Charles Linnington, 'Hay, Straw and Seed Merchant' (now the Swanage Christian Centre). However, Pouncy's original shop continued. Thomas Powell opened his studio on the corner of Station Road and Shore Road. Meanwhile, Walter Pouncy appointed a Mr Wild from Messrs Elliott and Fry of London to manage his Swanage business. The mobile studio on Shore Road was moved to Institute Road, and later to the lower High Street. Powell's new studio provided serious competition for Pouncy, and around 1904 another photographer, George Cox, opened a studio at 5 Institute Road. Pouncy closed his original shop in the High Street during 1905, although his 'Town and County Views' were still obtainable from the Misses White at 1 Institute Road.

Walter Pouncy's connection with Swanage and Purbeck continued as he owned a holiday property at Studland between about 1897 and 1911. Many of his later photographs featured Studland scenes and were reproduced as postcards. Several feature in the Purbeck Miscellany section. Although hampered in later years by increasing deafness, Walter continued to manage the Dorchester studio until his death on 1 October 1918. The business closed after nearly seventy-five years, and by 1920 Mrs Rose Bull was running a drapery shop on these premises.

Meanwhile, in Swanage, Thomas Powell had moved to a new studio on Shore Road around 1914. William had joined his father and, during the First World War, served on HMS *Achilles*. When Thomas Powell died, on 13 February 1921, William and his sisters inherited the studio. William's daughter, Norah (later Mrs Kaye), joined the business in 1927, and his son Alex followed in the mid-1930s. 'Powell's on the Sea Front' prospered, and perhaps best remembered are their photographs of the 1935 flood and the silver jubilee of George V.

William 'Bill' Powell served in the Home Guard during the Second World War, which was a busy time for the studio. He was awarded the MBE in 1951 for services to Swanage Lifeboat, and finally retired in 1956. In retirement he presented lantern slide lectures of his father's Old Swanage photographs. He died on 26 October 1973 aged 91.

Another photographer who provided competition to Powell was George Henry Cox (1875–1955). Cox was born to a farming family at Ottery St Mary, Devon. He was a real countryman and his early interest in fishing, shooting, the countryside and wild flowers continued throughout his life. He later specialized in wild flower photography. He was also a successful athlete. Cox came to Swanage and had set up a photographic studio at 5 Institute Road by 1904 under the trade name 'Ashford Cox'. The shop was run for many years by his American wife, Laura.

During the First World War Cox became a pioneer of aerial reconnaissance photography, serving with the Royal Flying Corps near Grantham. After returning to his Swanage studio he employed a young assistant named Murray Hardy in 1919, and Murray's sister, Jane (later Mrs Mason), joined the business in 1928.

Cox retired in 1930 and offered his vast glass negative collection to Murray who sadly declined, having nowhere to store them. (Murray subsequently worked for Randalls the Chemists and later for TRE at Worth from 1940–42.) Around 1942

Cox moved to Herston House (near the V.G. Stores), formerly the home of John Mowlem. Here he died on 7 December 1955 aged 80. His wife Laura died in 1962 and the large house remained unoccupied until its demolition during 1966/7, when Cox's collection of glass negatives was unwittingly destroyed. The floor was a 'sea of broken glass', although a few plates were rescued. We have included prints from two broken plates, showing the 1914 flood and the Gas Company c. 1920.

In 1929, the year before George Cox retired, a young lady named Helen Muspratt (1907–) opened a studio in Swanage. Helen and her sister Joan (1908–1958) were born in India where their father was serving in the Army. He retired to Swanage and his daughters were sent to Oldfeld School (now Harrow House). Helen later studied photography at London Polytechnic, while Joan became a teacher.

In 1928 Helen started work in London for Mr Donovan, a specialist in child photography. When she considered opening a studio Donovan suggested a seaside resort, and why not Swanage, which she already knew well. In 1929 the family moved above the shop at 5 High Street, near the Royal Victoria Hotel. Helen required a shop sign and approached Francis Newbery, former head of the Glasgow School of Art, who had retired to Corfe Castle. He also helped plan and organize the studio, which Helen ran on her own and later with Betty Tatchell.

The business moved to 10 Institute Road in the early 1930s, and by 1934 Joan had given up teaching and joined her sister. Helen later married and moved to Oxford, opening a studio under the name Ramsey and Muspratt. She became one of the leading women photographers of her generation. Meanwhile, Joan carried on the business at Swanage with Dorothy Horne and Cynthia Bradford.

With William Powell's retirement in 1956, Muspratt's became the only photographic studio in Swanage. Joan's sudden death in 1958 left only Dorothy Brunsdon running the business and it closed in December 1962. Helen Muspratt (now Mrs Dunman) retired to Cliff Cottage, her parents' home in Swanage.

This brings our story full circle, with John Rutherford opening his studio at 5 Kings Road East in 1963, and moving to 53 High Street in 1967. Two other photographers worthy of note are Arthur Stanley and Bruce Hibbs. Arthur George Stanley (1869–1951) was born at Sturminster Newton. He moved to Glastonbury and from 1883 served an apprenticeship under photographer Walter Tully. In 1888 he became a carpenter for John Merrick, who later sent Arthur to carry out work at Durnford School in Langton. He liked the area and stayed, marrying Eliza Stickland in 1902. From 1899 to 1951 Arthur ran a picture framing, photography, and carpentry business in the High Street at Swanage (opposite the Red Lion). Amazingly, this wooden studio still survived in 1991, as Smith's the greengrocers. Bruce Hibbs (1899–1981) was born in Swanage, and like George Cox joined the Royal Flying Corps, carrying out aerial reconnaissance photography. In the 1920s Bruce set up the Globe Studio at Belvedere, Swanage. He is perhaps best remembered, however, for running the newsagents (now Jenkins) from 1934 to 1973.

We hope you enjoy this nostalgic look at our home town and its surroundings. Its compilation has given us much pleasure.

David Haysom and David Bragg, 1991

SECTION ONE

# The Seaside

A TYPICAL EDWARDIAN BEACH SCENE. With the decline of the stone industry, Swanage was rapidly becoming a popular seaside resort, as shown by the facilities offered to the increasing number of visitors. Superior hotels, high class furnished apartments, beach huts, and yes, even a raft. (George Cox)

THE LAST ROSE OF SUMMER? The sands *c.* 1905, Cliff Cottage and 'Shiners' to the left. Development at the northern end of the beach was well established, with the Grand Hotel built in 1898 right of centre. (Rush & Warwick, Bedford)

ULWELL ROAD LEADING FROM THE SEAFRONT, *c.* 1905. The development at the northern end of the bay was now known as 'New Swanage'. The larger building, Sea Bank Lodge, still exists. The seats and drinking fountain provided by a thoughtful council have long since gone, replaced by commercial development now known as Ocean Bay. (The 'Wyndham' Series)

THE BEACH CAFE, NOW OCEAN BAY, *c.* 1912, then as now catering for holiday makers with a variety of goods and services. (The 'Ashfield' Series)

THERE IS NO DEVELOPMENT TO THE NORTH in this picture from 1870 and the sea wall has yet to be built, though the first bathing machines have appeared. In August 1877 George Stickland and George Clark, Bathing Machine Proprietors, were summoned by Joseph Parsons, Surveyor and Inspector of Public Nuisances to the Swanage Local Board, for allowing a 'bathing machine, appropriated for the use of Males, to be placed within 200 yards from a machine appropriated for the use of Females, contrary to the Bye Laws.' Mr Parsons stated that 'he saw several machines on the beach about two feet apart, they belonged to the defendants. He saw a lady get into one and a gentleman in the other and then they both bathed together. He saw George Stickland and told him he was breaking the Bye Laws, but he said he did not care.' Stickland and Clark were fined one shilling each and costs.

WHITE'S BATHING MACHINES, 1900. One section of the beach was set aside for gentlemen, one for ladies, and, to quote a local guide of the times, an area was set aside for 'mixed bathing', to show how broadminded the local authority had become.

JOHN DAVIS 'FASHION' WHITE, 1848–1927. A beach hut proprietor for over fifty years who also gave swimming lessons.

ANOTHER BUSY DAY ON THE BEACH, *c.* 1899. To the left is the Hibbs family home, and next to that The Cabin, now the Fisherman's Catch. John Braye's guidebook of 1890 described Swanage as 'an invigorating health resort', a 'family place where wives and daughters may safely be sent without being exposed to the extravagant vulgarities of many watering places, or the demoralizing atmosphere of the aristocratic rakes and loafers.' (Valentine's of Dundee)

DEVELOPMENT TO THE NORTH was rapidly continuing in 1910. To the left of centre was the open air concert pitch where, weather permitting, live entertainment was offered to visitors and residents alike. The sea wall had been constructed in 1904 and, though now illegible, the stone commemorating this event is set in the wall facing east. The wooden shelter on the right, which still survives, was built in 1908. (Photochrom Co. of London)

AN EARLY MORNING DIP in 1908.

THE RECREATION GROUND, 13 August 1908. A popular place for a picnic, now the site of the war memorial erected in 1920.

THE JUNCTION OF SHORE ROAD AND VICTORIA AVENUE, *c.* 1890. Stone bankers with the stone ready for shipment ran from the original Mowlem Institute to the stone quay. Pouncy's mobile photographic studio, used by Thomas Powell for daylight photography, can be seen on the right. (Thomas Powell)

THE SEAFRONT in 1902 and still no sea wall. (Walter Pouncy)

A BUSY DAY in the summer of 1925. The main part of the town clusters to the higher ground on the southern end of the bay. The groynes are in course of construction as can be seen by the two pyramid structures just left of centre. (Francis Frith & Co.)

PUNCH AND JUDY in the 1950s, a popular and traditional entertainment for children and adults alike. (Eric Bichard)

ERNEST BRISBANE, 'conjuring, ventriloquism and Punch and Judy. Lynford, The Hyde, Langton Matravers. Available for parties,' c. 1960.

THE CABIN TEA ROOMS in the 1920s. Now altered and refurbished, it is known as the Fisherman's Catch.

A TRIP BY CHARABANC ALONG THE SEA FRONT around 1926. R.H. Barrett was the driver. Dean & Barrett and Russell Parsons had stands for charabancs allocated at Folly Knap, between the Pier and the Royal Victoria Hotel Gardens and on Shore Road. Dean & Barrett started a bus service to Herston in July 1924 but two years later the *Swanage Times* announced that 'owing to complaints as to the noise of the motor-tram the services to Herston have been suspended.' The 'motor-tram' was then acquired by Russell Parsons and put to work on the seafront running from the Pier to the Beach Café (now Ocean Bay). The driver was C.S. Bennett and the vehicle can be seen in the next photograph.

NOT ALWAYS A VISITOR'S PARADISE. High seas during 1926. Russell Parsons' 'motor-tram' can be seen in the background, on the extreme left. (William Powell)

AN UNUSUAL SIGHT anywhere along the south coast. This waterspout in Swanage Bay was caught by camera in the late 1930s. (Alex Powell)

A GENERAL VIEW in the 1930s. In the foreground the old concert pitch has gone, to be used as a site for ice cream vendors. A landing stage runs out from the beach for passengers embarking on one of the many and varied trips on the 'Gondoliers'. (Valentine's of Dundee)

AN AERIAL VIEW OF THE CENTRE OF THE TOWN before the Second World War and the building of the De Moulham estate. The bandstand can be seen to the left of the picture, now as then a popular venue for band concerts and art exhibitions. (Aero Pictorial Ltd)

JUST PRIOR TO THE SECOND WORLD WAR illuminations were festooned along the seafront, sadly for one summer season only, the feeling being that the town should not end up as a second Blackpool. (William Powell)

## SECTION TWO

# The Piers, Tramway and Stone Bankers

A PHOTOGRAPH OF THE FIRST PIER taken around 1899. Built in 1859, this was mainly a working pier, goods such as coal, timber and fish being transported along the tramway which ran inshore to The Parade. To the right is the Wellington Clock Tower, brought from London in 1867 and still standing today, though minus its spire and somewhat obscured by recent residential development. The paddle steamers are the *Monarch* (left) and the *Empress*. (The 'Wyndham' Series)

STONE BANKERS, *c.* 1875. Stone was transported from the quarries and banked up awaiting shipment by sea. These piles of stone were called 'bankers'. The stone was loaded into high-wheeled carts which were driven into the sea, off-loaded into rowing boats or 'lighters', taken out to deeper water and transferred into ketches for final shipment. (B.J.K. Rives)

STONE BANKERS from the Mowlem Institute towards the Tourist Information Centre, *c.* 1880. The 'Black House', the front of which was destroyed in a storm, is just right of centre. It stood at what is now the north end of The Parade. (Francis Frith & Co.)

WORKED STONE AWAITING SHIPMENT opposite the Royal Victoria Hotel (now turned into flats), at the lower end of the High Street, *c.* 1880. (Francis Frith & Co.)

LONGSHOREMEN AND IDLERS BY THE QUAY, *c.* 1900. On the right is fisherman Tim Hopkins who would stand and yarn for an hour or more without taking the lobster pot off his back. Seated left is 'Carrots' Hixson who was noted for the horsehair fishing line which he braided up himself. The fisherman in the centre smoking a pipe is Jimmy Pond. (Thomas Powell)

ON THE QUAY, 1929. Charlie Brown on the left and Johnnie Brown on the right show off one of the last good catches of herring to a couple of locals. (Helen Muspratt)

FISHERMEN NEAR THE QUAY. Tommy Marsh is on the left, with 'Bidgee' Hixson and Jack Hixson.

THE LOWER HIGH STREET TOWARDS THE PIER, 1907. Jock Macrae is at the wheel of one of the Swanage Motor Company's vehicles advertised below.

# SWANAGE MOTOR COMPANY

**LIMITED.**

HIGH STREET [Near the Pier].

**Telephone No.: 75.**

Ten-Seater Char-a-Bancs as above for Private Parties. Any Distance.

*Touring Cars and Landaulettes.*

Char-a-Bancs to Lulworth, Bournemouth, etc.,

THE NEW PLEASURE PIER, *c.* 1906. This was constructed in 1896. Horse-drawn carriages await fares from passengers disembarking from the paddle steamers *Brodick Castle* (left) and *Lord Elgin*, while cattle graze on what was to become the miniature golf course. (George Cox)

AN EARLY POSTCARD, from around 1905, of the pier approach. Marine Villas (centre) still exists, while the Hotel Grosvenor had yet to reach its full potential. (Valentine's of Dundee)

A BUSY SUMMER'S DAY, *C.* 1900. Paddle steamers regularly plied between Bournemouth and Swanage. The horse-drawn carriages were popular with visitors wishing to see places of interest such as Durlston Castle and the Great Globe. (Thomas Powell)

A GENERAL VIEW LOOKING WEST TOWARDS THE TOWN, *c.* 1890. The pier tramway can be seen in the centre, and ran from the bankers (now The Parade) to the end of the 'old' pier. The tramway was designed by Captain W.S. Moorsom, chief engineer of the Southampton and Dorchester Railway, and built in 1859. It was originally intended to connect with the quarries in the 'parishes of Langton Matravers and Swanage,' but due to opposition from local residents and landowners in Swanage only the initial section was built. The tramway was constructed to standard gauge with the intention of joining with the London and South Western Railway, should a line be built from Wareham. No locomotives were permitted in the vicinity of houses in Swanage under the terms of the Swanage Pier and Tramway Act and consequently horses were used to move the loaded wagons. However, little stone was carried by the new tramway as the stone merchants were unwilling to pay the tolls imposed. The pier was frequently criticized in the local newspapers as easterly gales regularly broke away large sections. The stone merchants continued to load stone in the traditional way, which involved manhandling the stone up to five times before the loaded ketches sailed to London and beyond. A coal and fish store was built at the town end of the tramway in the late 1880s, after the railway line from Wareham had been built and the stone merchants had moved their bankers or stone yards to the new station yard. With the construction of the new pleasure pier in 1896 the tramway was simplified and re-gauged throughout to the narrow gauge of 2 ft 6 in. It was used for coaling up the paddle steamers until the outbreak of the First World War. Isolated sections of the tramway were used until the 1930s and some parts still survive today. (Valentine's of Dundee)

LEADING TO THE PIER ENTRANCE, *c.* 1895. The bearded gentleman was Walter Prouten, reputed to have caught the 'last' smuggler. The lady to the left was a Miss Burt. (Thomas Powell)

THIS SCENE SHOWS THE FIRST TOLL-HOUSE AT THE PIER ENTRANCE, *c.* 1885. The standard gauge tramway running parallel with the High Street from the pier to The Parade can be seen. It was converted to narrow gauge after the new pier was built in 1896 and sections of it can still be seen today.

THE ORIGINAL 'OLD' PIER, *c.* 1880. The rowing boats in the foreground are pulled up on Buck Shore in front of what is now Swanage Sailing Club. The loading cranes on the pier were removed during the 1880s when the number of paddle steamers plying between Bournemouth and Swanage increased. (Francis Frith & Co.)

WORKING BOATS ALONGSIDE THE 'OLD' PIER, *c.* 1903. In the background is the Grosvenor Hotel, formerly a private house known as The Grove.

THE PADDLE STEAMER *MONARCH* berthed at the 'old' pier in July 1902. This steamer was built in 1888, operated by Cosens and Co. for many years, and scrapped in 1950.

A BEVY OF BEAUTIES. Left to right: *Victoria*, *Majestic* and *Monarch* alongside the 'old' pier, c. 1910, ready for coaling up from the pier tramway. This practice ceased with the outbreak of the First World War.

THE SECOND OR 'NEW' PIER, c. 1900. It is now in a state of considerable disrepair, only certain sections being open to the public.

EXTENSIVE WORK TO THE NEW PIER was undertaken in 1928, making good the ravages of the sea, and here the work force poses for posterity. Back row, left to right: -?-, 'Bidgee' Hixson, Tim Edmonds, Alf Sadler, Frank Legg, -?-, Albert Bowering. Middle row: -?-, George Stevenson (diver, later piermaster), Edward Brunsden (piermaster). Front row: Tom Wright (?), Harry Hibbs (?). (William Powell)

THE HOTEL GROSVENOR in 1927, still developing. This photograph shows work progressing on the western end. Did the seaplane bring one of the hotel's more affluent visitors?

A POPULAR VIEW in the 1930s. In the foreground is the miniature golf course, while the paddle steamers *Monarch* and *Bournemouth Queen* are tied up alongside the pier. (Valentine's of Dundee)

MARINE VILLAS to the landward end of the pier, *c.* 1865. Salt water baths formed part of the building until 1855. Is the carriage waiting for a wealthy visitor or guest? (Isaac French)

THE GROVE, *c.* 1885. Originally a private residence, it was extended and refurbished in 1892 and again in 1902 to become the Hotel Grosvenor.

LOOKING WESTWARD FROM THE DOWNS, *c.* 1899. Between the Wellington Clock Tower (originally a monument to the Duke of Wellington, and brought piecemeal from London in 1867) and the Lifeboat House are the original fishermen's huts, now replaced. The council-owned boat park was yet to be developed. The paddle steamers berthed at the two piers are, left to right: *Empress*, *Monarch* and *Lord Elgin*? (The 'Wyndham' Series)

THE PADDLE STEAMER *EMBASSY* tied up at the 'new' pier in June 1966. Built as the *Duchess of Norfolk* in 1911, she was used extensively on the Bournemouth to Swanage run and even as far afield as Torquay. In 1938 she was rebuilt and renamed the *Embassy*, and is seen here during her last summer season before being scrapped in April 1967. On the gangway is Jack Ward (son of Alfred Ward), who acted as agent for the paddle steamers from 1946 until they were withdrawn in 1966. (Chris Phillips)

THE PADDLE STEAMER *MONARCH*, a regular visitor in the 1920s. Development towards 'New Swanage' was still sparse but, as can be seen, building continued apace at the northern end of the bay. (Bruce Hibbs)

LOOKING TOWARDS PEVERIL POINT, *c.* 1900. The lifeboat slipway had yet to be constructed. Towards the Point is the property known as Waterside, while between that and the Lifeboat House are the Old Watchhouse and Coastguard Cottages. (Francis Frith & Co.)

AN EARLY PICTURE OF THE BATTERY at Peveril Point, *c.* 1880, ready to repel any invader.

FIRING PRACTICE AT PEVERIL POINT, 1905. The local Volunteers (No. 5 Company 1st Dorset R.G.A.) won the King's Cup at Shoeburyness in that year.

'THE LOOKOUT', PEVERIL POINT, *c.* 1904. Today a somewhat more modern structure is manned by the local Auxiliary Coastguards. (T. Carey & Co., Swanage)

SECTION THREE

# Wreck and Rescue

THE WRECK OF THE *NETTO*, Peveril Ledges, 1900. The Norwegian brigantine *Netto*, carrying a cargo of salt, was driven ashore in a violent south-easterly gale. The skipper later told William Powell that, confused by poor visibility, he was under the impression they were rounding the Isle of Wight, but in fact were rounding Durlston Head. She struck about noon; by six o'clock she had broken in half and the stern was washed ashore. The captain, the four crew and the ship's cat were brought ashore by breeches-buoy, the cat being taken to Powell's home. (Thomas Powell)

THE LAUNCHING CEREMONY OF THE *WILLIAM ERLE*, 28 December 1890. She was Swanage's second lifeboat, but the crew found her unsatisfactory, and she was never launched on service, being replaced in August 1893.

THE SECOND *WILLIAM ERLE* , *c*. 1905. She replaced the earlier boat at a cost of £584. She was on station until May 1914, saving fourteen lives. Tragedy struck on 12 January 1895 when coxswain William Brown was lost overboard on her second launching. (T. Carey & Co., Swanage)

THE WRECK OF THE *DIANA*, Durlston Bay, 1 April 1922. The ketch *Diana*, carrying a cargo of Jersey granite, was disabled when her mainsail tackle broke off Peveril Ledges and she drifted ashore in Durlston Bay. The rocket apparatus saved the captain, his wife, son and crew.

LAST VOYAGE OF THE LIFEBOAT *HERBERT STURMY*, 1928. Left to right: Arthur Dyke, Bill Dyke (coxswain), Charlie Brown (second coxswain), Frank Inman, Bob Brown and Harry Bartlett (standing). The *Herbert Sturmy* was replaced by the *Thomas Markby* in June 1928. (William Powell)

THE *THOMAS MARKBY*, the first motor lifeboat, December 1938. Back row, left to right: Frank Inman jun., Johnnie Brown, Ken Hardy, Frank Inman sen., Trevor Chadwick, Alf Chinchen, Arthur Dyke, George Coffin, Jim Hardy, 'Siddy' Marsh. Seated: Bob Brown (second coxswain), William 'Bill' Powell (hon. secretary), W.S. Field, Edgar Millward and Charlie Brown (coxswain). (Alex Powell)

THE WRECK OF THE *MAUD MARY*, January 1939. This vessel, carrying a cargo of bricks and sailing under the Polish flag, was abandoned in the English Channel. The crew of three men and a woman escaped in the 'small boat' and eventually reached Weymouth safely. (William Powell)

ARRIVAL OF THE NEW LIFEBOAT *R.L.P.*, 26 February 1949. The *R.L.P.*, a 41 ft 'Watson' class non-self-righter costing £15,584, replaced the *Thomas Markby*. Left to right: Bill Dyke (on the slipway) and Charlie Brown (behind the rudder). On the boat: Alf Chinchen (motor mechanic), Lew Hardy (second coxswain), Bob Brown (coxswain), Mr R.R. Cousins (RNLI inspector), Doctor de Jersey (Chairman RNLI Swanage Branch), G. Mooring Aldridge and J. Butler (committee), Johnnie Brown (bowman), Frank Inman, Ken Hardy (signalman), Reg Marsh and Freddie Pond. (Joan Muspratt)

THE *R.L.P.* ON THE SLIPWAY, 1949. The slipway was constructed in 1928 to accommodate the first motor lifeboat, the *Thomas Markby*. Extensive alterations were also made to the boathouse. Launchers Bill Dyke and Charlie Brown are on the slip. (Eric Bichard)

LAUNCHING THE *R.L.P.* on an Inspector's Exercise, 1949. Mr R.R. Cousins (RNLI inspector) is standing aft. The first service launch of the *R.L.P.* came on 4 September 1949 when the coastguard reported sighting distress flares off Lulworth Cove. However, despite a thorough search, nothing was found. The Weymouth lifeboat eventually found the disabled yacht *Lilida* with her three crew and took the vessel in tow. The first life-saving service by the *R.L.P.* came on 16 April 1950, when a Vampire aircraft crashed into the sea 7½ miles south of Durlston Head. The pilot had parachuted into the sea and was saved by the lifeboat which later transferred him to a naval Motor Torpedo Boat. During her 26 years on station the *R.L.P.* answered 341 calls and saved 242 lives. She was replaced in October 1975 by the *J. Reginald Corah*, a 'Rother' class self-righter costing £95,000. The paddle steamer seen in the background of this photograph is the *Bournemouth Queen*. This was her penultimate season on the Bournemouth–Swanage run before being transferred to Southampton in 1951. She had been rebuilt in 1946 and was scrapped in 1957. (Eric Bichard)

SECTION FOUR

# Snow, Fire and Flood

THE GREAT SNOW STORM of 25 April 1908. The building to the right, rebuilt in 1908, for many years Eardley Brooke's estate agents office and recently The Galley, was the birthplace of William Masters Hardy, the author of *Old Swanage and Purbeck*. (George Cox)

SWANAGE'S FIRST FIRE ENGINE, *c.* 1900. This was given to the town by George Burt and housed in the basement of the Town Hall. Below: the brigade on the way to a fire with this first appliance loaded onto a horse-drawn cart. (Thomas Powell)

THE FIRE SERVICE in 1908. The new horse-drawn appliance was aptly named *The Swan*. In the background is the relatively new police station, completed in 1899. (Thomas Powell)

ON PARADE AT THE JUNCTION OF COURT ROAD AND KINGS ROAD, *c.* 1916. Back row, left to right: Mr King, the driver (Anchor Inn), F. Bennett, F. Moss, A. Summers. Front row: H. Gallop, H. Chinchen, W. Vaughan. T. Day, M. Lloyd, F. White, F. Bishop, J. Goater, W. Chinchen, R. Goater. The cyclists were messengers, presumably proceeding to the fire either to say that the brigade was on its way or, possibly, 'keep the fire going till they arrive.'

PARRY'S FIRE, 15 June 1914. Samuel Parry's ironmongers shop was badly damaged in this dramatic fire. Sailors from a ship anchored in the bay assisted with salvage work, throwing stock out from the rear of the building. However, it is said that they broke more items than were rescued intact. Arthur Stanley's wooden studio can be seen on the right, and he can be glimpsed in the crowd. His career is described in the introduction. Stanley ran this picture framing, photography and carpentry business from 1899 to 1951 and, amazingly, the studio still survives as Smith's the greengrocers. It was originally built as a cycle store for Mr Lambert Rose in 1897. (Thomas Powell)

THE CREW OF THE *WHITE ROSE* POSED FOR POSTERITY, *c.* 1931, in Kings Road, opposite St Mary's parish church. Back row, left to right: E. Langdon, P. Foot, F. White, R. Hoptroff, H. Chinchen. B. Mathews. Front row: S. Pitcher, H. Goodchild, F. Stockley, H. Gallop, W. Vaughan, C/O C.A. Colmer.

THE WEDDING OF PETE DOREY AND MARJORY DAY, 27 January 1931, at the Congregational Chapel, High Street, now the United Reformed Church.

THIS PARTICULAR FIRE APPLIANCE, converted by the members of Swanage Fire Brigade from an old Daimler, purchased from Haysome's garage (and not paid for), gave sterling service from 1932 onwards. It is seen outside the Swanage Steam Laundry, now Swanbrook Mews.

ON DISPLAY OUTSIDE THE ROYAL VICTORIA HOTEL in the mid-1930s. Note the 'home-made' Daimler fire appliance on the right.

ARGYLE ROAD, 28 May 1934. A recurring scene; road works in progress frequently led to the tar sprayer catching on fire. (William Powell)

THE SAME SCENE FROM A DIFFERENT ANGLE. A small boy's delight, 'where there's smoke there's fire.' (William Powell)

A FULL COMPLEMENT. Retained firemen and the Auxiliary Fire Service (AFS) on parade in 1944 at the entrance to King George V playing fields. Back row, left to right: A. Selby, A. White, -?-, P. Brennan, F. Brown, L. Mills, H. Gallop. W. Burt, J. Legg, A. Norman, J. Orchard, F. Damer, T. Langtree, W. Mitchell, R. Wilson, H. Woodhouse, R. Norman, T. Keates, A. Galton, W. Squibb, D. Brown, W. Chinchen. Front row: T. Cowdrey, B. Marsh, G. Ballam, J. Perry, T. Stickland, F. Summers, P. Foot, E. Langdon, S. Pitcher, H. Chinchen, T. Rolf, C. Colmer, V. Bennett, D. Bending, J. North, D. Squibb, A. Phippard, J. Stares, L. Goater, -?-. (Joan Muspratt)

THE CANDLEWICK FACTORY BLAZE, 5 September 1966. This was the largest fire in Swanage for many years and destroyed Ronald Boot's Candlewick factory and part of John Curtis' antique shop in the High Street (opposite the United Reformed Church). The Swanage Fire Brigade was joined by appliances from Wareham and Hamworthy, but low water pressure at times reduced the flow of water through the hoses to a trickle, slowing down the fire-fighting operation. (John Rutherford)

'FIRE DRAMA AT FACTORY' was the headline in the *Swanage Times* on 7 September 1966. The paper reported that, 'Swanage fire service under station officer R.E.J. Paull dealt with the seat of the fire in the boiler room and latex processing department. But it had got a hold on the high roof of Curtis' antique showrooms by 12 noon. A volunteer chain gang carried furniture and materials from the factory and house into the Labour Hall. Just before 1 p.m. the fire burst out of the upper windows of Curtis' building fronting the High Street, sending showers of hot stones and plaster into the street.' The fire raged for over four hours and damage was estimated at £100,000. On the right John Aplin's shop (demolished in 1972) can also be seen. (John Rutherford)

THE FLOODS of 9 March 1914. Eldon Terrace, one of the lower lying parts of Swanage. (Thomas Powell)

PUMPING OUT FLOOD WATER FROM JIMMY DAY'S SHOP, 10 March 1914. This is now the Alliance and Leicester and Lloyds Bank next door is now the National Westminster. One of the boys, Vic Harding, recalls that the picture was taken before they went to school on the day after the flood. This photograph by George Cox was printed from a broken glass plate rescued from Herston House (the home of the photographer). His career is described in the introduction. Left to right: Mr White (Giddy's father), Mr Reynolds (owner of the wine shop), Capt. 'Giddy' White, Cecil Harding, Vic Harding, George Weekes (man at bank door), Sidney Shelston, Fred Moss, Fred Bennett, Arthur Summers.

THE GREAT SWANAGE FLOOD, Kings Road, 17 November 1935. The post office is now on the left. (William Powell). Below: the junction of Spring Hill and Kings Road. The boat is manned by, left to right, Freddie Pond, PC 'All Aboard' Long, Bill Dyke. (Randalls – Murray Hardy)

KINGS ROAD EAST FROM THE HIGH STREET, another view of the 1935 flood. (William Powell)

THE HIGH STREET LEADING TO THE SQUARE. On the extreme left was Ashlar House which was demolished in 1938. It is now the site of Swanage Library. (William Powell)

STATION ROAD. The 1935 floods were possibly the most extensive in the history of Swanage. To the left there is now Woolworths, then the Central Garage. (William Powell)

THE AFTERMATH. Pumping out flood water in Station Road. To the left is the Dorothy Café, now Boots the Chemists. (Joan Muspratt)

THE SQUARE in the floods of 1935. The buildings are virtually unchanged today with the exception of Swanage Dairies to the left which was destroyed by bombing on 17 August 1942. (William Powell)

'NIAGARA FALLS'. Flood water pouring from The Square over the sea wall by The Parade in 1935. (William Powell)

OUTSIDE THE CONSERVATIVE CLUB, Kings Road, 14 September 1962.

EFFORTS ARE MADE TO BUILD A DAM in Kings Road in 1964 to divert flood waters from Eldon Terrace and Kings Road East. In the background is the site of the Health Centre, then used as coal yards. (John Rutherford)

ELDON TERRACE, 3 February 1990. With the implementation of the Flood Alleviation Scheme, hopefully this may be the last time such photographs can be taken. (Lisa Lambeth)

VICTORIA AVENUE, at the junction of Northbrook Road, on the same day. (Lisa Lambeth)

SECTION FIVE

# The Town Centre

PANTON'S BREWERY, *c.* 1870. This view was taken before the building of the railway from what later became Station Road. James Panton's brewery and the manager's house are seen in the centre. The brewery was taken over in 1893 by Strong's of Romsey, who removed all the plant and stock. It was subsequently demolished, and in 1899 the London and South Western Railway extended their goods yard sidings. This is now the site of the Health Centre. The 'brook' is seen before it was straightened and channelled under the shops on the south side of Station Road.

OVERLOOKING THE TOWN CENTRE, FROM THE HIGH STREET, *c.* 1870. To the extreme right is the Mowlem Institute, and in the centre Brook Farm and Dairy (now the site of Barclays Bank). Woolworths' present site is obscured by a small clump of trees to the left. Between Brook Dairy and the Mowlem Institute is the old smuggler's cottage seen in the next photograph. (B.J.K. Rives)

THE OLD SMUGGLER'S COTTAGE, Station Road, *c.* 1905. In William Masters Hardy's book, *Smuggling Days in Purbeck*, an amusing anecdote is related concerning a smuggler and customs officer living 'cheek by jowl'. This resulted in the smuggler being caught red handed. The cottages were demolished in 1914 to allow road widening and subsequent redevelopment.

THE SMITH FAMILY, Station Road, *c.* 1882. Captain Smith and his wife lived in the cottage shown in the previous photograph. They are seen here with their two daughters and five sons – a sixth, Fred, was in Australia. The sons are, left to right: Frank (fisherman), Alfred (master mariner), Hugh (builder), Tommy (bricklayer) and Harry (mariner, who also ran the fish shop in Station Road).

STATION ROAD, LOOKING WEST, *c.* 1910. A rare view showing, on the left, Lloyds Bank, built in 1906 (now the National Westminster), and Thomas Powell's photographic studio on the right. The corner of Station Road and Shore Road was redeveloped in 1914 and is now 'K's' Eating House, formerly Fortes.

THOMAS POWELL (1860–1921), 'Photographic Artist', *c.* 1910. The successful businessman outside his studio (seen in the previous photograph). Powell had opened this studio in 1898 after acting as manager for photographer Walter Pouncy at his shop in the High Street. His career is described in the introduction. It is to this gentleman that we owe the remarkable photographic record of 'Old Swanage' that he captured with his home-made camera, consisting of wood from old cigar boxes and a lens which cost 4s. 6d., a tidy sum in those days.

THE 'NEW SHOPS' IN STATION ROAD, 1908. Road widening took place later and the cottages on the left, including Brook Farm and Dairy, were demolished. Would present day hygiene regulations allow a butcher's display of this kind?

FRISBY'S BOOT STORES, Station Road, *c.* 1908. The staff stand proudly outside the shop, which survives as a shoe shop today. Frisby's offered 'Boating, Tennis and Golf Boots' with 'low shoes for summer wear and bar shoes for the promenade.' All goods were 'marked in plain figures at keen prices' and 'if your boots require repairing send a postcard, and we will fetch, repair and return them same day if necessary.'

# Gilbert Hall Pictures

## KING'S ROAD, SWANAGE

(3 MINUTES FROM STATION).

Lessees ... ... THE SOUTHERN CINEMA Co.

GENERAL MANAGER - - D. H. CURTIS.

UP-TO-DATE PICTURES WELL SHOWN.

OPEN NIGHTLY ALL THE YEAR ROUND AT 8.

Entire Change of Programme Three Times Weekly

**MONDAY, WEDNESDAY, FRIDAY.**

THE GILBERT HALL, Kings Road (latterly the Church Hall), c. 1914. This was the first cinema in Swanage and operated from around 1912 until the opening of the new Electric Theatre (now Gateway) in June 1916. The film advertised above was the 1912 Italian silent version of *Quo Vadis?*. The Gilbert Hall was also used for shows and the short-lived roller skating craze of 1908–12. Admission cost 6d. during the day and 3d. in the evenings, with skate hire at 6d..

THE STAFF OF THE GILBERT HALL PICTURES, c. 1912. Back row, left to right: Charlie Linnington, Frankie Parker, Tom Sidnell (manager), Gerry Stockley (operator/projectionist), Freddie Cooper. Boys in front row: Bert Bradford, ? Sidnell (Tom Sidnell's son), Edward Stockley (Gerry's brother). A number of the staff, including Gerry Stockley (sole operator/projectionist), transferred to the new Electric Theatre in Station Road when it opened in 1916. The hand-cranked projection equipment, previously sited in the gallery of the Gilbert Hall, was also moved to the new cinema.

SWANAGE GAS COMPANY, Station Road, c. 1920. This photograph was taken by George Cox, and has been printed from one of the broken glass plate negatives rescued from Herston House during demolition in 1966/7. Unfortunately, the majority of this priceless collection of Old Swanage negatives was unwittingly destroyed.

GENERAL VIEW OF STATION ROAD, *c.* 1925. This photograph, looking towards the old Mowlem Institute, shows the Swanage Cinema and The Grand Theatre on the left. The history and development of these places of entertainment is shown and described in the following photographs. The Gas Company offices in the previous picture can be seen on the extreme right. This corner of Station Road was destroyed by enemy bombing on 20 April 1942 during the raid which also devastated Cornwall Road. (Owen Hardy)

THE SWANAGE PAVILION, Station Road, 1919/20. This interesting photograph shows the conversion of the Swanage Pavilion from a former army hut used for shows during the First World War. The performers included Freddy Beck and Dorrie Dean. (Owen Hardy)

THE SWANAGE PAVILION, *c.* 1923. It was renamed The Grand Theatre, and in 1932 the owner, Mr F.A. Walton, converted it into a cinema. In 1936 Walton sold out to Portsmouth Town Cinemas who submitted an elaborate scheme to rebuild The Grand in the art deco style, but this was rejected due to planning difficulties.

THE GRAND CINEMA, *c.* 1937. Next door was the Central Garage, with the Lugano Ballroom above. In April 1953 Tony Whitehouse took over both cinemas and in November of that year closed The Grand. It became the Ritz Ballroom after partial rebuilding. This was short lived however, and it became the dress shop, 'Louise', which was incorporated into the Gateway supermarket following closure in the early 1980s.

THE SWANAGE CINEMA, Station Road, 1930. Left to right: Gerry Stockley (chief operator/ projectionist), Dick Mayo (second operator) and George Holmes (rewind boy). This is now the Gateway supermarket. The cinema originally opened as the Electric Theatre in June 1916. Dick Mayo recalls that 'I joined as a Rewind boy in June 1919 at about 15s. a week.' The silent era came to an end when Warner Bros released *The Jazz Singer* with Al Jolson in 1927 but, as Dick Mayo remembered, 'I didn't think sound would last.' Dick became manager under Portsmouth Town Cinemas, serving until Tony Whitehouse bought the cinema in April 1953 and renamed it the Ritz. The growth of television saw cinema audiences decline, however, and in 1959, projectionist Bob Dwen recalls, 'Tony Whitehouse told the staff that if business did not improve the cinema would close at the end of the season. The weather that summer was extremely good, so at the beginning of October we closed and Whitehouse turned it into the supermarket.'

ADVERTISEMENT FOR THE SWANAGE CINEMA, *c.* 1923. The 1920s were the great days of the silent cinema. Dick Mayo recalls the 1921 version of *The Four Horsemen of the Apocalypse*, starring Rudolph Valentino: 'I saw it thirty times. The owner of the cinema, Mr Walton, actually hired a fellow named Miller who did all the special effects at the Empire Cinema in London, and kept him in Swanage for a week. Walton got Raymond Senior to read the prologue. He would walk on the stage all dressed in black and say "I am the prophet John." It was marvellous.'

THE QUEUE FOR THE SWANAGE CINEMA on a rainy afternoon in August during the 1930s. Dick Mayo recalls that 'in the summer we had queues past the Railway Hotel and the other way round into Mermond Place.'

SWANAGE CARNIVAL PROCESSION, *c.* 1935. The Carnival Queen and her attendants are seen passing the original Mowlem Institute, where Billy Sutton and his Savoy Follies were entertaining audiences every afternoon and evening. To the left was the departure point for the Southern National Omnibus Company's service to Weymouth.

DEMOLITION OF THE MOWLEM INSTITUTE in 1965. The building incorporated the local library and a lecture hall visited by 'First Class Concert Parties'. The popular show of the 1950s and '60s, 'Each Evening', is well remembered. (David Bragg)

SECTION SIX

# The Railway

THE STATION YARD AT SWANAGE, *c.* 1902. Adams Radial tank '415' class No. 428 is seen shunting an interesting variety of London and South Western Railway wagons. This locomotive was built by the LSWR in 1883 and withdrawn in 1925. Stacks of stone can be seen in the background, where the bankers or stone yards had been transferred from the seafront after the opening of the railway in 1885. The goods yard closed on 4 October 1965, although two sidings were retained for coaching stock purposes until 6 June 1967, when the signal box was also closed and subsequently demolished. (Thomas Powell)

ARRIVAL OF THE BRANCH TRAIN FROM WAREHAM, 1896. An Adams '02' class tank No. 208 is seen approaching Swanage station with a mixed rake of LSWR oil-lit coaches dating from the 1860s and '70s. This locomotive was built in 1891 and transferred to the Isle of Wight in 1930 where she was renumbered as No. 17 and named *Seaview*. She was withdrawn in 1966, although No. 209 (later renumbered No. 24) *Calbourne* is now preserved at Havenstreet on the Isle of Wight Steam Railway, the only member of the class to survive.

'DAD IN THE SIGNAL BOX', 1899. Tom Purchase, Swanage's first signalman, at work in the 24 lever box which survived until 1967. Note the bird cage (centre top). The budgie no doubt provided company for Tom during his working day. Most of the early railway photographs in this section are from the collection of Mrs Kay Webb (a relative of Tom Purchase) who has kindly donated them to the Tithe Barn Museum.

AN EXTERIOR VIEW OF THE SIGNAL BOX in 1899. This poor (but rare) early photograph was taken from an open LSWR wagon (full of manure?). Signalman Tom Purchase (left) stands on the balcony, which was later altered with the addition of a porch.

SWANAGE STATION on a fine summer's day in 1896. A Beattie single-framed goods loco (possibly No. 347) brings an excursion train of LSWR gas-lit six-wheelers into the main platform. The original goods shed can be seen on the left with an LSWR road van outside. The cross-over to the bay platform was taken out of use on 16 December 1945.

THE STATION YARD FROM THE CHURCH TOWER in 1897. This interesting view shows a wide variety of LSWR wagons. The goods shed in the centre was extended to its present length in 1898. Note also the stacks of worked stone or bankers and the wooden-railed cattle dock. In the background, new hotels, boarding houses and private residences have been built in Gilbert Road, Ilminster Road and Cranborne Road. (Francis Frith & Co.)

A BUSY DAY AT SWANAGE STATION, *c.* 1908. Every line is occupied as special trains prepare to depart taking troops home after one of the annual Volunteer tented camps at 'New Swanage'. These were held for many years until the outbreak of the First World War in 1914, when permanent wooden barracks were erected. The fine array of locomotives includes an Adams 'A12' class in the main platform and a Drummond 'K10' on a double-headed train in the bay platform. The coaching stock is equally varied.

THE FIRST SIGNALMAN. Tom Purchase poses for posterity around 1905. He was interviewed in 1935 (aged 78) on the fiftieth anniversary of the opening of the railway. 'I signalled the first train out of Swanage. The driver was, I believe, Fred Stickland and the fireman Bill Longman of Bloxworth. The relief station master was George Parsons from Portland, and the first guard was Fred Young. The assistant signalman was Fred Barnes of Wimborne. William Howe was head porter and Harry Clark warehouseman.'

THE FIRST STATION MASTER. George Parsons was station master from the opening of the railway in 1885 until his retirement in 1903. He is seen here with a guard around 1900.

HAYSOM'S POSTING STABLES in Court Road, *c.* 1900. In a few short years the motor car would render these horse-drawn carriages obsolete, although the building itself survived until 1979. On the left is Henry Burt's stone yard (later Haysom and Sons' stone depot).

A RARE VISITOR, July 1938. LMS 4–4–0 No. 628 on the turntable after working an excursion from Bristol and Bath via the Somerset and Dorset. This class of loco was introduced in 1928 and upon nationalization in 1948 was taken into British Rail ownership. Withdrawal of the class began in 1959 and was completed by 1962. (S.C. Townroe)

THE GREAT SWANAGE FLOOD, 17 November 1935. The station yard, like much of the town centre, was affected, the water almost reaching platform level. This scene was repeated on 3 February 1990, although the station is now the home of the Swanage Railway Project, who have fought to gradually rebuild the Swanage branch since its closure on 3 January 1972.

THE HEYDAY OF THE SWANAGE BRANCH. Drummond 'M7' No. 30106 shunts empty stock in August 1953. During the immediate post-war years and throughout the 1950s the Swanage branch once again flourished. However, the increase in private car ownership would soon bring this prosperity to an end. (R.R. Bowler)

ON THE TURNTABLE, August 1954. Drummond '700' class No. 30695 was a familiar sight at Swanage during the 1950s, working mainly goods traffic and carrying out general shunting duties. Built for the LSWR in 1897, she was finally withdrawn from Bournemouth shed in December 1962. (R.R. Bowler)

DRUMMOND '700' CLASS NO. 30695 approaches Victoria Avenue bridge with the 9.24 ex-Swanage service in August 1953. It was unusual for a member of this class to be seen on a passenger working. The stock comprises an ex-LSWR three-coach set and later Maunsell stock. (R.R. Bowler)

A DRIVER'S EYE VIEW OF CORFE CASTLE STATION. This was taken in August 1953 by Mr R.R. Bowler from the cab of a Drummond 'M7' on a branch train to Wareham.

'BATTLE OF BRITAIN' CLASS NO. 34109 *SIR TRAFFORD LEIGH-MALLORY* enters Corfe Castle station on 8 August 1953 with a Maunsell eight-coach rake on a through train to London Waterloo. The locomotive was originally built at Brighton works in 1950 and in common with other members of the class was later (1961) rebuilt, with the air smoothed casing removed. She was withdrawn in September 1964. (R.R. Bowler)

*SIR TRAFFORD LEIGH-MALLORY* RECEIVES THE 'RIGHT AWAY' on the same day, while 'M7' No. 30106 waits at the 'Down' platform with the branch 'push-pull' for Swanage. (R.R. Bowler)

ADAMS RADIAL NO. 493 RACES THROUGH CORFE CUTTING with a train to Bournemouth Central around 1903. This locomotive was built in 1884 and originally based at Exeter. She was later transferred to Bournemouth shed and withdrawn in 1921. The Adams Radial tanks (4–4–2) worked for many years on the Lyme Regis branch, and No. 488 (BR No. 30583) is now preserved on the Bluebell Railway. (Thomas Powell)

NEAR WORGRET JUNCTION, August 1953. 'M7' No. 30112 crosses over to the main 'Up' line with a branch goods train from Swanage and Corfe Castle. The Drummond 'M7' tanks (0–4–4) saw many years service on the Swanage branch until 1964. Although this particular engine was withdrawn in February 1963, two members of the class still survive today. One of these, No. 30053, was shipped to the USA in 1964, but has since been repatriated and is now based on the restored Swanage Railway. (R.R. Bowler)

A RARE SIGHT at Wareham station on 15 August 1953. LMS diesel electric locomotive No. 10000 on trials. This was the first main line diesel locomotive in Britain, built at Derby in 1947. No. 10000 later returned to the Midland Region and, until withdrawal, was chiefly confined to fast freight work. (R.R. Bowler)

ANOTHER VIEW OF DIESEL ELECTRIC NO. 10000 leaving Wareham on the same day, assisted by a Maunsell mogul. (R.R. Bowler)

'BATTLE OF BRITAIN' CLASS NO. 34072 *257 SQUADRON* prepares to depart from Swanage station on a wintry afternoon in February 1991, as the past is recreated on the restored Swanage Railway. This locomotive was built in 1948 and withdrawn in 1964. However, she was rescued from Woodham's scrapyard at Barry, South Wales and restored to running order in only eighteen months. (David Haysom)

SECTION SEVEN

# The High Street

THE HIGH STREET, c. 1904. Parry's the ironmongers, which continued trading until September 1988, is on the left. Biggs Wine Merchants, on the right, purveyed fine wines and spirits.

THE LOWER HIGH STREET, *c.* 1906. On the right stands the Royal Victoria Hotel. Hixson's House Agency, Brown's fish shop and the original Steam Packet Office (extreme right) can also be seen. They were replaced in 1908 by new development. (Walter Pouncy)

COSENS AND CO.'S STEAM PACKET OFFICE, 1922. Alfred Ward (1869–1941), their agent from 1898 to 1941, stands outside. This building was formerly Charles Burt's Stone Office and included a weighbridge. It has recently been rebuilt and extended.

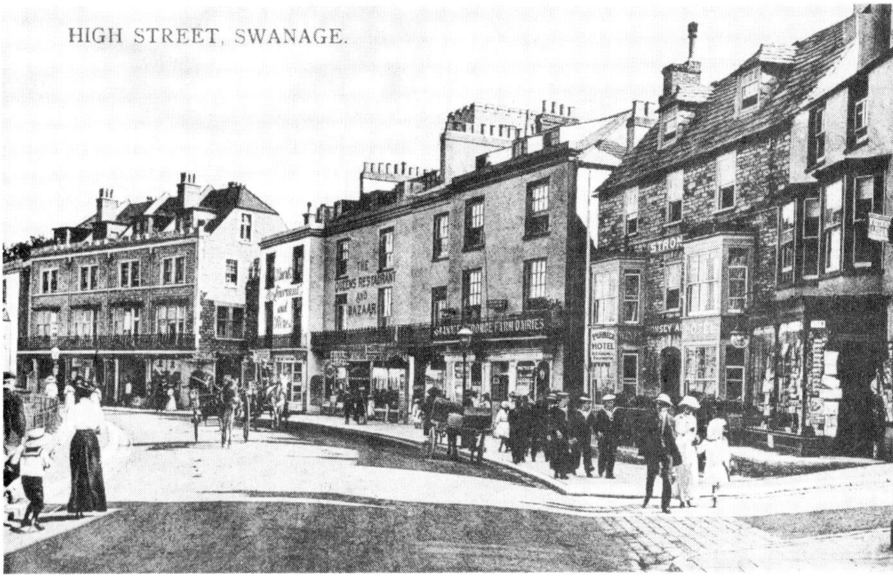


VICTORIA TERRACE, *c.* 1909, the home of John Mowlem after his retirement to Swanage in 1844. The Purbeck Hotel, to the right, still survives. Between this and Burt's Lane stood Swanage Coombe Farm Dairies, the Queen's Restaurant and Bazaar, and Burt's Restaurant and Stores. (Dorset Series)

THE SWANAGE GARAGES, DEAN AND SON, June 1930. This garage (opposite the Purbeck Hotel) was built with special wooden roof trusses constructed by George Hardy, the well known local builders. It later became Sheasby's South Dorset Coaches and still survives, although in a dilapidated condition. Dean and Son's advertisement of 1934 offered 'Sun Saloon Motor Coaches (Maroon & Grey) – Tours to Beauty Spots of the South. Booking Office for Motor Coaches to all parts of England and Wales.'

THE SQUARE, *c.* 1905. To the right stands the 'Round House', which was demolished in 1929, while on the left stands The Swanage Dairies, surmounted by a golden calf.

THE SWANAGE DAIRIES, *c.* 1910. A close up of 'Ye Olde Dairie' in The Square, then run by Messrs Dean and Curtis, later managed by the much respected Harry Smith. The dairy was completely destroyed by enemy action on 23 August 1942. The golden calf (made of wood) was blown onto the roof of a building opposite.

THE FIRST POST OFFICE, THE SQUARE, *c.* 1900. This occupied premises next to The Swanage Dairies. The first postmaster, George Horlock, is seated in the carriage. The post office moved to Station Road around 1907, and the original premises later became Bick's the tobacconist. Today the site between the White Swan and Taunton Road is occupied by a variety of different businesses. (Thomas Powell)

THE SQUARE, *c.* 1920. The Trocadero Restaurant, run by the Misses West, was well known and patronized by both locals and visitors, for whom a cream tea at the 'Troc' was a must. Below: a general view of The Square from an upstairs window of the Trocadero. The lamp post in the centre bore a sign: saying 'Motor cars drive slowly'. (Miss Bertha Potter)

THE HIGH STREET LOOKING WEST, 1896. The Anchor Inn (extreme right) survives largely unchanged, but Dixon's the confectioners gave way to a new bank for R. Williams and Co. (now Lloyds Bank) in the year this photograph was taken. In the background Walter Pouncy's new photographic studio is under construction, incorporating large windows and a special skylight. This was named The Arcade, and Thomas Powell acted as manager until he set up his own studio in 1898, when Pouncy closed this new shop. It was taken over by Charles Linnington, 'Hay, Straw and Seed Merchant' and is now the Swanage Christian Centre. However, Pouncy's original shop (seen in the next photograph) remained in business until 1905. (Thomas Powell)

FURTHER ALONG THE HIGH STREET, *c.* 1903. On the left is Pouncy's original studio, opened in January 1888, where Thomas Powell was manager. On the extreme right was Charles Smith the blacksmith and, beyond, the wooden studio used by Arthur Stanley for his picture framing, photography and carpentry business from 1899 until his death in 1951. This shed was originally built as a cycle store for Lambert Rose in 1897 and, amazingly, still survives as Smith's the greengrocers. (The 'Wrench' Series)

PARRY'S, 'THE MODERN IRONMONGERS', *c.* 1920. Samuel Parry surveys the High Street. He opened the business in 1890 and it continued trading until September 1988.

THE RED LION PUBLIC HOUSE in 1882. Opposite is King Alfred Place, built by Sir John Charles Robinson in 1876. The cottages protruding on the right occupy the site of the present Town Hall.

THE TOWN HALL, C. 1890. There was not so much traffic congestion when all the vehicles were horse-drawn. (Walter Pouncy)

THE OLD CURIOSITY SHOP, C. 1935. This was opposite the Town Hall and was at one time Tim Hopkins' fish shop. It was demolished as recently as 1959 and is now the site of Burr Stone Mead, a residential development. (William Powell)

THE TOWN HALL AND VIRGINIA COTTAGE in 1955. This view shows the ornate front of the Town Hall, originally the façade of the Mercers' Hall in London, built in 1670 and brought to Swanage in 1882.

WESLEY'S COTTAGE opposite Purbeck House (now The Convent), *c.* 1938. This cottage was so called because John Wesley stayed here for one night in 1774. A popular tourist attraction, it was destroyed by enemy action on 14 May 1941. (Joan Muspratt)

'THE NARROWS', *c*. 1905. This was one of the narrowest sections of the High Street but, following bombing in the Second World War, is now one of the widest. The entrance to Chapel Lane is on the left, and the large building was The Albany Restaurant Rooms, which also provided accommodation for cyclists. The Narrows and Chapel Lane were largely destroyed by enemy bombing during the raids of 17 August 1942 and 3 February 1943. However, most of the buildings on the right survived, including the Barley Mow.

'THE NARROWS', *c.* 1928. 'Pete' Coffin is seen crossing the road. The poster site on the right advertises entertainments at The Grand Theatre in Station Road. The majority of these properties have since been demolished. (William Powell)

G. GREEN, BUTCHER AND GROCER, *c.* 1906. The proprietor George Green (left) with his son Bill Green (centre) and an assistant pose for posterity. This building is now the Methodist Lounge (previously Two Wheels).

THE FIGURE HEAD, c. 1875, at one time a well known coffee tavern in 'The Narrows'. The Day Centre now stands on this site, set back from the road. (B.J.K. Rives)

TATCHELL'S BOOT SHOP, c. 1880. The business later moved to larger premises (now Bourn Art Galleries), and then to Institute Road before closing in 1989.

'THE NARROWS', *c.* 1928. 'Pete' Coffin is seen crossing the road. The poster site on the right advertises entertainments at The Grand Theatre in Station Road. The majority of these properties have since been demolished. (William Powell)

THE TOP END OF 'THE NARROWS', *c.* 1905. This is just below Magnolia House, leading to Church Hill. The buildings on the right were built in 1888 and still survive.

AT THE TOP OF CHURCH HILL, c. 1905, leading to the Black Swan. The Palgrave memorial cross, erected in 1909, now stands on the site of the town pump. Church Hill House is seen before the extension was added. (Arthur George Stanley)

OLD TOWNSEND LANE, c. 1906. These buildings no longer exist and Townsend Road, a wide thoroughfare, now leads to Queens Road and the Cottage Hospital. (Arthur George Stanley)

ST MARY'S PARISH CHURCH, *c.* 1885. The clock face was moved from the east side of the tower to the west around 1900 in order to serve new residential development in that part of the town. The ring of four bells was increased to eight in 1888, the gift of George Burt as a memorial to his late wife Elizabeth.

THE MILL POND, *c.* 1870. A few original properties remain. Around 1880 a wall was constructed as a safety measure for those overindulging at the Black Swan. It has been said that strangers falling into the Mill Pond qualified as locals when they came out.

CHURCH BRIDGE, *c.* 1880. The cottages have since been demolished to allow the main access to St Mary's parish church off Church Hill. To the left was a watering place for horses. Note the clock face in its original position on the eastern side of the tower.

ST MARY'S PARISH CHURCH from Northbrook Farm, *c.* 1870. With the exception of the tower, the church was rebuilt during 1859/60. The cluster of cottages in the centre has given way to attractive lawns and flower beds. (B.J.K. Rives)

PRIEST'S WAY, leading to the Mill Pond, 1884. In the distance are St Mary's parish church and the old Mill House. Kings Road was not yet built and Argyle Road is now on the right, where the new police station was erected in 1899. On the extreme left the railway station was in the course of construction. (Francis Frith & Co.)

THE BLACK SWAN, c. 1875. With the exception of the public house, little remains of this section of the High Street. To the right is now Townsend Road while, on the left, Church Hill leads to Kings Road. (Walter Pouncy)

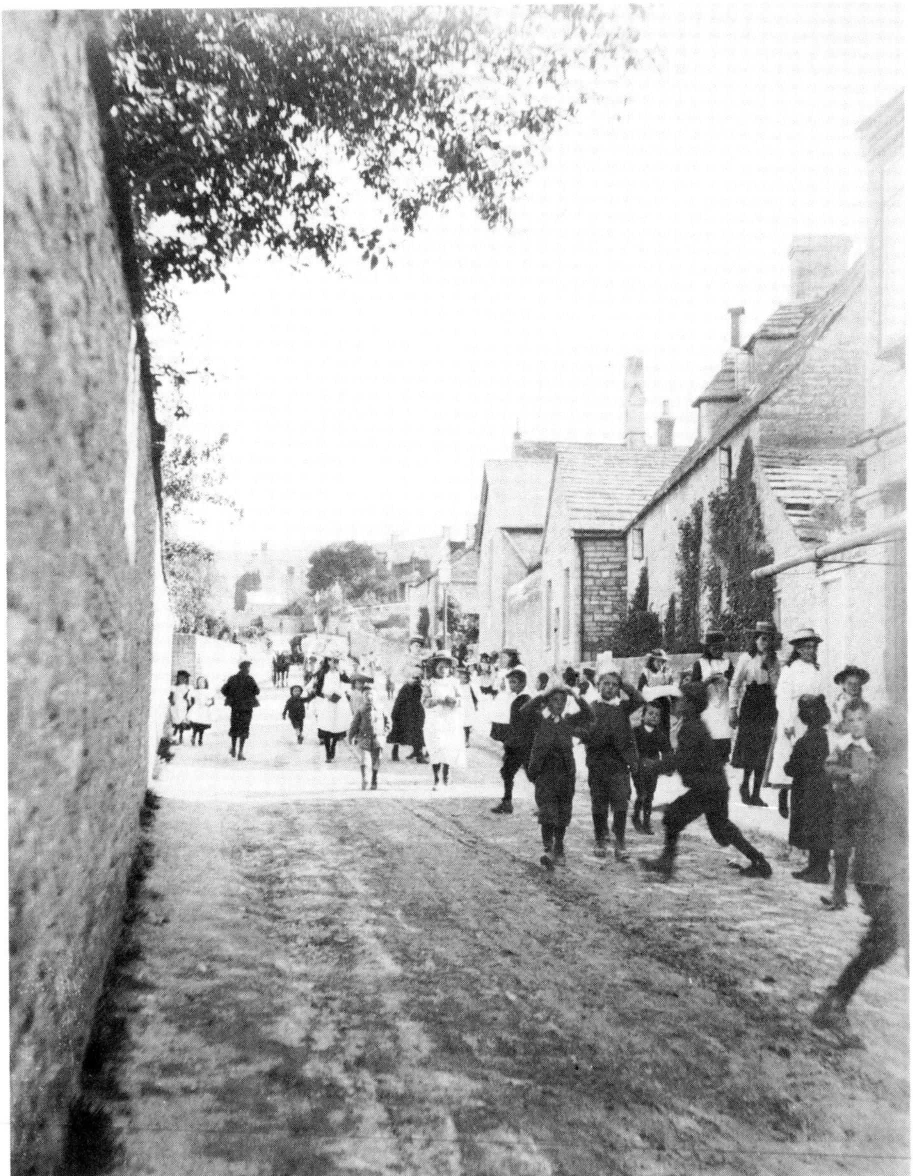

BELL STREET, HERSTON, July 1901. 'School's out'. Parents still pick up their children from the same school and, except for variations in dress, a similar photograph could be taken today.

BELL STREET, c. 1875. Some of the cottages on the left survive. The grassy bank on which the children are sitting now leads through to Jubilee Road. (B.J.K. Rives)

HERSTON SCHOOL in 1914. The school had recently been extended, as shown in this postcard view taken by Arthur George Stanley, whose career is described in the introduction.

SECTION EIGHT

# Quarrying

GEORGE 'BOSSY' BURT'S QUARRY at Townsend, *c.* 1891, with Sammy Norman (left) and 'Single' Dowland. The horse has been disconnected from the 'spack' and is attached to the quarry cart. The beam at the top of the 'slide' was to prevent cattle from falling down the shaft. (Thomas Powell)

ANTHONY HAYSOM (left), great grandfather of the co-author, with Billy Dowland (seated) and two younger members of the Haysom family, *c.* 1900. (Thomas Powell)

CHINCHEN FAMILY QUARRY, *c.* 1900. This quarry was situated on part of what is now Priest's Way caravan site. The boy is seated on the quarry cart. Other members of the Chinchen family are standing with possibly the most important member of the group, their stalwart horse.

A TYPICAL QUARRY, C. 1900. Many quarries were damp, and heavy rains and poor drainage made for very difficult working conditions. These men are gathered round the barrels – perhaps for a little light refreshment?

A DAY OFF? Harry Chinchen, aged 13, on the family horse. Most of the quarrying photographs in this section are from the personal collection of Jack Chinchen (Harry's son), who has kindly allowed these family pictures to be included.

HARRY CHINCHEN (right) AND WALTER BROWN at Cowlease with their faithful donkey, *c.* 1920. This is now part of the Hoburne Park estate. The capstan can be seen in the centre and the loaded quarry cart stands at the top of the 'slide'. This quarry was previously worked by the Squibb family. In the background can be seen 'the scar bank' of stone chippings forming part of the hill known as 'grandfather's knap'.

HARRY CHINCHEN (left) AND WALTER BROWN AT WORK, C. 1920. The donkey is 'walking the circle', harnessed to the 'spack' which is attached to the capstan. The quarry cart has just reached the top of the 'slide'. If the capstan chain was removed and the donkey continued to 'walk the circle', it would still step over the point where the chain would normally be.

A CLOSE UP OF HARRY AND WALTER, C. 1920. A pigeon loft is attached to the quarry 'house'. The donkey looks well cared for, but which one was the pigeon fancier?

UNDERGROUND AT COWLEASE, *c.* 1920. Harry and Walter show a visitor their place of work. This is a 'good ceiling', although the height of a 'lane' could vary from 8 ft or more to as little as 3 ft, making life extremely difficult for the quarrymen.

ABOVE GROUND, *c.* 1920. Harry and Walter show their visitor one of the quarry 'houses', with a quarryman working stone on one of the 'bankers' or work benches.

A FAMILY PORTRAIT, *c.* 1920. Harry Chinchen with his dog and the faithful donkey.

TAKING A BREAK, *c.* 1920. Harry and Walter pose for a photograph with Harry's sister Annie.

'THE DEPOT', COURT HILL, *c.* 1930. Harry and Walter are displaying a mason's 'mark' on a stone pave. This is now the council yard at the junction with Kings Road.

HAYSOM AND SONS, STONE DEPOT, COURT HILL, *c.* 1930. Back row, left to right: Sam Florence (from Hamworthy), Fred Lock, Fred Haysom (father of the co-author), Phil Brown. Middle row: Walter Haysom (standing), Bert Tomes, Albert Phippard, Arthur Bonfield, John Haysom, Jimmy Chinchen, Harry Phippard, Bert Norman. Front row: Frank Haysom, Harry Gillingham, Albert Haysom, Charlie Coleman, Harry Tomes, Teddy Corben, Arthur Corben, Sid Cooper.

## SECTION NINE

# People and Events

JOHNNIE GOTOBED ('GO-TO-BED'), (1820–1900), a well known Swanage character. His parents kept a public house in the High Street, but Johnnie branched out on his own, first as a carrier and then as a coal merchant. In later years he lived in a little cottage in 'Hop-About' Lane (the lower section of Queen's Road).

JOHN MOWLEM (1788–1868). Born in Swanage, he founded Mowlem, the well known construction firm in London which still carries his name. After his retirement to Swanage in 1844 he took an active part in parish affairs, contributing much to the town. Most important was the original Mowlem Institute built in 1863 and redeveloped in 1965 as 'The Mowlem', a lasting memorial.

GEORGE BURT (1816–1894), a nephew and partner of John Mowlem. In 1875 he rebuilt Purbeck House (now The Convent) for his retirement. Burt was also responsible for many improvements to the town, carrying on Mowlem's excellent work. These included finally bringing the railway to Swanage in 1885, the gasworks, fresh water, a drainage system and many 'bits and pieces' of old London transported as ballast in the stone boats. The author Thomas Hardy once described him as 'the King of Swanage'. (Maull & Fox, London)

'THE GREAT GLOBE', c. 1890. Constructed at Mowlem's stone yard at Greenwich in 1887, it is now situated at Durlston Head. It weighs some forty tons and consists of fifteen sections, yet another of George Burt's many unusual contributions to his home town.

WALROND ROAD, 12 September 1910. 'All my own work.' At the junction of Walrond Road and the seafront there is not a mechanical digger in sight. (Thomas Powell)

THE SNOW FLAKE MINSTRELS, 1905, a popular local group of the day. Back row, left to right: Fidler Bower, Jack Clark, John Stickland, Charlie Redout, Arthur Welsh, Morris Longman. Front row: Tommy Whitfield, Harry Tatchell, Frankie Parker, Moses Grant, Jack Parker.

MISS JULIA COLSON (1830–1916). Quite a character. She wore a crinoline to the last, green glasses, elastic-sided boots and white stockings. An enthusiastic youth worker, she ran Bible classes and was secretary of the Shipwrecked Mariners' Society. On one occasion she came into church, saw the top hat of a retired Admiral on the font, and sent it flying with her umbrella, saying 'that's not the place for a hat.' William Powell once offered a young fellow a pound of tobacco if he would stand in front of Miss Colson and take a photo, but he refused to risk it.

THE OPENING OF THE CHILDREN'S HOSPITAL, Steepways, 31 October 1919. In the centre are Thomas Hardy and the Bishop of Salisbury, Dr Ridgeway. Also in the group are Dr Ll. A. Baiss, Col. Balguy BRRC, Mrs Cecil Hanbury BRRC, Lady Ilchester, Matron Miss Dymond and Sister Bramwell. (Arthur George Stanley)

SWANAGE COUNCIL SCHOOL INFANTS, Mount Scar, 1922. Back row, left to right: Len Clark, Harry Stockley, Eddie Inman, ? Backhouse, Jack Lovell, Jack Trim, Jack Herne, Bill Selby, Teddy Masters. Middle row: Margery Taylor, Barbara Strong, Ada Hancock, Cissie Lovell (behind), Arthur Hancock, Alf Snook (?) (on horse), Jack Trent, Iris Vye, Marie Strickland, Betty Green, Mary Parsons. Front row: Gladys Lemon, Kathleen Crowther, Dolly Carter, Elsie Ridout, Florrie Bishop, Kitty Purchase, Barbara Bastable, Olive Francis, Evelyn Burgess, Doris Churchill.

THE FIRST 'SKYWAYMEN' SQUADRON, Herston School, 1936. 'The Flying Club of which Mr H.C. Comben, an ex-RAF pilot, who served in the Great War, is the leader. All the boys are enthusiastic members of the *Boy's Own Paper* flying league, and derived great benefit from Mr Comben's expert instruction. Good flying, Herston!' Standing, left to right: Lennie Mansfield, Harry Comben (teacher), Ted Churchill, Jack Grant, Fred Grant, Mr Butler (headmaster), Ron Summers. Seated: John Dennis, Joe Powell, Fred Riley, Doug Williams, Sam Bonfield, George Farr, Leonard Alner, Dennis Richardson, Frank Tomes, Ted Langdon. Front: Eric Smith, Gerry Roff.

DURLSTON COURT SCHOOL, 1938. The first XI cricket team. The captain in the centre is none other than 'the Lad Himself', Tony Hancock (1924–1968). His parents ran a hotel in Bournemouth, and the future radio and television comedian was sent to Durlston Court School between 1931 and 1939.

SWANAGE BRICKWORKS, c. 1930. The Swanage Brick and Tile Company was established in 1861 and still survives today. Among the group are: Mr Codling (top left), Frank Frampton, Frank Andrews, Tommy Williams, Charlie Diffey, 'Jacko' Diffey, Jack Mortimer and Charlie Reynolds.

TAKING IT EASY, NEAR THE QUAY, c. 1950. Left to right: 'Siddy' Marsh, Mr Butler, 'Bidgee' Hixson, Harry Brown, George Summers, Mr Emerson, David Lloyd-Davies (?).

SILVER JUBILEE OF GEORGE V, 6 May 1935. The elaborate jubilee decorations in Institute Road. Councillor J. Smith presented propelling pencils to the children at Herston School and the Council School, Mount Scar. The 'stop me and buy one' ice cream vendor was a familiar sight in the 1930s. The Westminster Bank (left) was destroyed by enemy action on 17 August 1942. (William Powell)

THE JUBILEE BEACON, NORTH HILL, 6 May 1935. This was one of many which stretched across the country. The beacon was lit by boy scouts at 10 p.m. and was made up of old tyres, some of which later rolled down the hill while alight. In Swanage a firework display took place on the recreation ground. (William Powell)

CORONATION OF GEORGE VI, 12 May 1937. Crowds gather round a maypole by the Mill Pond. An Old Peoples' Tea and Entertainment was held at the Church Hall, Kings Road on Thursday 13 May. (William Powell)

THE CORONATION DECORATIONS, 12 May 1937. A view of the High Street, including the Town Hall and the old cottages opposite. There was two way traffic in those days, and no parking problems. (William Powell)

VIEWS OF THE CORONATION DECORATIONS, 12 May 1937. Swanage was acknowledged as one of the best decorated towns along the south coast on this royal occasion. The High Street (above) is little changed, but in Station Road (below) many shops have changed hands, and the Swanage Cinema (later the Ritz) gave way to the supermarket in 1959. (William Powell)

SECTION TEN

# The Two World Wars

THE OLD FIRE STATION, Kings Road, *c.* 1943, sandbagged and ready for action, with Freddie Summers 'on duty'. A small tobacconists and sweet shop occupied the left-hand side of the building, although both cigarettes and confectionery were in short supply.

TROOP TRAIN AT SWANAGE STATION, c. 1918. Troops, possibly on their way to the front, bid farewell to their loved ones. Throughout the First World War the purpose-built camps at 'New Swanage' were used extensively for training exercises. (Bruce Hibbs)

SWANAGE STATION FORECOURT, c. 1916. Horses and Limbers assemble and the troops are mustered before marching to the camps at 'New Swanage'. The goods yard sidings on the right had been lengthened in 1899 and remained in position until 1967. This is now the site of the Health Centre.

'YOUR COUNTRY NEEDS YOU', *c.* 1916. Troops marching down the High Street (just below the Town Hall) during the First World War.

'THE CAMP' (now Ballard Estate), 1915. This was one of five camps built by Parsons and Hayter and George Hardy for MacDonald Gibbs and Co. (supervising engineers to the War Department) during 1914/15. These camps extended west towards the Swanage Brick Works and Godlingston. (George Cox)

FIRST WORLD WAR AIRCRAFT in fields below Oldfeld School (now Harrow House) during October 1918. These unique photographs show sentries patrolling the two planes. Nearest to the camera is a Sopwith F1 Camel (F9417), which first flew at No. 3 Western Aircraft Repair Depot on 30 September 1918, before going to No. 3 Training Depot Station (TDS). It crashed on 8 November 1918 and was written off. The second is an Avro 504K (D9321), one of a batch produced late in the war by Parnell and Son of Bristol and fitted with a 'camera gun'. Three of its companions later became civil aircraft.

MESSERSCHMITT 109E of 5/LG2 crash landed, owing to engine failure, at Woodyhyde Farm, Harmans Cross, near the railway line, on 28 November 1940. The pilot, Paul Wacker, was taken prisoner. The tailplane of this machine is now incorporated in one of the Royal Air Force exhibitions periodically on display at Hendon.

HEINKEL 111 G1–BH of KG 55 crashed at Westfield Farm, Studland on 25 September 1940 at approximately midday. It was returning from a bombing raid on the Bristol Aircraft Factory at Filton. One crew member died of wounds, the others were eventually sent to Canada for the rest of the war. The pilot, Feldwebel Fritz Jurges, visited the site in May 1977 and has since spent holidays in Swanage.

von **Swanage** über die Bucht von Swanage auf die hohen Kliffs an der **Handfast Point**

TWO RARE SECOND WORLD WAR GERMAN RECONNAISSANCE PHOTOGRAPHS. The top view was reproduced from a pre-war photograph, judging by the vantage point.

THE RUINS OF LULWORTH CASTLE. It was not the victim of enemy action but had been destroyed by fire in 1929.

REHANGING THE BELLS of St Mary's parish church, 1940. The ring of eight bells was rehung by Taylor's of Loughborough at a cost of £394 10s. 0d. Due to the wartime ban on the ringing of church bells (except in the event of an invasion) the newly rehung bells were not rung until Sunday 14 November 1942, after the Allied victory at El Alamein. They were not rededicated until 18 September 1943. (Capt. J.B.M. Ridout)

ST MARY'S RING OF EIGHT BELLS awaits transportation to Taylor's foundry at Loughborough during the rehanging work in 1940. The three smallest bells were recast, and also the seventh bell (dated 1621) which was found to be cracked. The oldest surviving bell in the tower today dates from 1594 and was cast by John Wallis of Salisbury, whose career lasted nearly fifty years. He was a most successful bell founder and around 250 of his bells survive in Wiltshire, Dorset and the surrounding counties. (Capt. J.B.M. Ridout)

THE HOME GUARD, Priests Road, 1944. Back row, left to right: Bert Collier, Bill Redout, Chris Bradford, Tom Wright, Bob Spearman, Bill Fowler. Front row: Malcolm Pond, George Aplin, Bill Laird, Fred 'Bud' Green, Jack Satherley, Bob Cann. (William Powell)

BOMB DAMAGE IN CORNWALL ROAD after the air raid of 20 April 1942. Considerable destruction was also caused in Station Road. Total casualties were five killed and twenty-one wounded. (Ray Hibbs)

PARK ROAD following the bombing raid of 13 July 1942. Casualties included three wounded.

AIR-RAID PRECAUTIONS BUREAU, protected by sandbags, in Shore Road, 1939; now the Tourist Information Centre. (William Powell)

THE SQUARE, showing the remains of The Swanage Dairies and the Ship Hotel, following the raid on 23 August 1942. Casualties were five killed and nine wounded.

INSTITUTE ROAD after the air raid of 17 August 1942. The Westminster Bank (left) was completely destroyed, and Haymans and Muspratt's photographic studio damaged. This raid also affected Chapel Lane and destroyed a large part of 'The Narrows'. The overall casualty figures were eight killed and thirty-nine wounded. (Joan Muspratt)

'SALUTE THE SOLDIER WEEK', 1–8 July 1944. On the platform at Swanage station. (William Powell)

'THE NARROWS' AND CHAPEL LANE following clearance after the raids of 17 August 1942 and 3 February 1943. This is now the site of the Day Centre and Swanage Youth Club, although the cottages opposite still survive. 'The Narrows' had in fact been scheduled for slum clearance during the late 1930s. (William Powell)

THE TITHE BARN, Church Hill following the raid of 3 February 1943. A bomb fell in the old churchyard and seriously damaged cottages in Church Hill and the roof of the parish church. By 21 January 1944 the total of air raid alerts in Swanage totalled 929, compared to 700 in London, an interesting fact not generally known.

REMOVING ANTI-INVASION DEFENCES, 21 August 1944. The sappers are preparing the way to clear the beach of mines, while workmen start to dismantle the tubular scaffolding defences. (James Jeffrey)

THE SEAFRONT, summer 1945. 'Getting back to normal', although some evidence of the war can still be seen, including the concrete 'dragon's teeth' anti-tank defences and tubular scaffolding. (Ray Hibbs)

BOMB DAMAGE AT CHURCH HILL caused by the raid of 3 February 1943. The cottages were subsequently demolished and this is now the site of the 'new' Rectory. (William Powell)

VJ DAY, 15 August 1945. The Japanese surrender marked the end of the Second World War. The flag at St Mary's parish church was flown at half mast, and the Last Post sounded by Arthur Goodey (verger and parish clerk) in remembrance of those who gave their lives in the war. The bomb damage to the roof of the church can be clearly seen, and a total of fourteen windows were blown out.

SECTION ELEVEN

# Purbeck Miscellany

HAYMAKING NEAR CORFE CASTLE on a summer's day around 1895. A traditional rural scene, far removed from the mechanical methods employed today. (Walter Pouncy)

THE SQUARE, CORFE CASTLE, July 1901. To the left is The Greyhound and on the right The Bankes' Arms, both of which have survived the ravages of time.

CORFE CASTLE seen from East Street, July 1901, a favourite viewpoint. With no motorized traffic, life was more leisurely.

THE STATION APPROACH, *c.* 1905. A flock of sheep, possibly on its way to Wareham market? (Photochrom Co. of London)

CORFE CASTLE STATION, *c.* 1904. An excursion train to Swanage approaches the 'Down' platform. The locomotive, Adams '460' class No. 477, was built in 1884 and withdrawn in 1927. The station survives and has been restored by the Swanage Railway Project. (J. Welch and Sons, Portsmouth)

CORFE CASTLE VILLAGE, *c.* 1900, viewed from Challow Hill overlooking the village. The scene is little changed today apart from the residential development to the rear of West Street. (Walter Pouncy)

A TYPICAL VILLAGE SCENE in West Street, *c.* 1930. This was once the main street, and in medieval times the Purbeck marble industry flourished here. (William Powell)

WORBARROW BAY, *c.* 1935. This is now part of the Army firing ranges and, sadly, these cottages no longer survive. This card was posted at Tyneham in 1936, seven years before the Army took over the village. (Sunray Super Series)

KINGSTON VILLAGE, *c.* 1905, a scene virtually unchanged today. The Scott Arms is on the right, with Lord Eldon's magnificent 'new' church to the left. This was designed by G.E. Street and built between 1874 and 1880 using local stone and timber. The ring of eight bells, cast by Taylor's of Loughborough, is one of the finest in Britain. (Dorset Series)

THE VILLAGE POND, WORTH MATRAVERS, *c.* 1875. Ducks on the pond were at one time declared a 'health hazard' by the local authority. (B.J.K. Rives)

WORTH MATRAVERS VILLAGE, *c.* 1868. A rare early view showing the church of St Nicholas before its extensive restoration between 1869 and '73. A pyramid roof was added to the tower and the three bells rehung by Warner's of Cripplegate. (B.J.K. Rives)

THE SQUARE AND COMPASS, c. 1913. It is little changed today, and the same family still offers refreshment to weary travellers.

T.R.E. AT WORTH MATRAVERS, 1940. A rare official photograph of the wartime Telecommunications Research Establishment, where much of the early pioneering work on radar was carried out. T.R.E. moved to Malvern in May 1942 when the threat of bombing raids increased.

*HEDBURY QUARRY*, by H.T. Wells RA. Thomas Chinchen Lander is standing centre. His two sons Albert and Thomas are in the foreground. Cliff quarrying had largely died out by 1850.

HEDBURY QUARRY after closure, *c.* 1885. A fine view of the 'whim' or derrick of a type probably used in other cliff quarries including Tilly Whim. (Walter Pouncy)

THE HARRIS QUARRY at Winspit, *c.* 1950. This was worked in its final years by Bob Harris and closed in the late 1950s. (Joan Muspratt)

QUARRY AT LANGTON, *c.* 1900. A typical quarry at work. The donkey has just drawn the loaded quarry cart to the top of the 'slide'. The capstan and quarry 'houses' are also seen to good effect. (Walter Pouncy)

THE KING'S ARMS, LANGTON, *c.* 1895. Alfred Masters takes the rein of his lead horse after most probably having 'bin in somewhere' prior to driving his team with their stone wagon down to Swanage. (Thomas Powell)

PARSON'S BARN near Studland, *c.* 1913, a large cave used by smugglers for hiding contraband. The roof collapsed during the severe winter of 1962/3. (Walter Pouncy)

THE *STUDLAND BELLE*, *c.* 1913. Built as the *Advance* in 1904, she was acquired by Messrs S.P. Shippick in 1912 and used briefly on a Boscombe–Bournemouth–Studland service. She was the first sabbath breaker, landing passengers at Swanage on Sunday 3 August 1913. She was destroyed by fire in the winter of 1913/14.

THE PINNACLE, Studland, July 1913. The postcard reads, 'This is one of the tall rocks at the back of the cliffs. I took the Photographer (Walter Pouncy) out in the boat to take this just over a week ago. You can see me standing by the end of the cliffs. Am just off on the beach for the day. Yours etc, Walter – 9 am 28/7/13.'

THE *GRACE DARLING*, c. 1911, owned by Isaac Masters and used to bring coal at 16s. a ton from Poole to Studland. His son, F.W. Masters, is seen by the bow of the rowing boat, and Arthur Tubb (?) aboard the *Grace Darling*. (Walter Pouncy)

OLD STUDLAND COTTAGES, *c.* 1905. This postcard was sent from Swanage to Mr H. MacDonald, Shepherds Bush, London on 27 July 1909. It reads, 'Dear Mac, We arranged to go to Studland today but as last year is wet. Have you arranged any matches at Lord's. What date is last Test at Oval. England doing rotten as usual, going to get whopped (thrashed) in both of them most likely, Phil.' Nothing changes! (The 'Wyndham' Series)

AN AEROPLANE AT STUDLAND, *c.* 1930. This light aircraft (wings removed) was owned by Cyril Berens (on the extreme left of the photograph), son of the artist Alexander Berens. In the centre George King, owner of the petrol pumps (also Agglestone Stores), is seen 'filling up' the aircraft. The Methodist chapel can be seen in the background.

FIRE AT STUDLAND DAIRY, 8 August 1908. This photograph was taken by Walter Pouncy while spending a summer holiday at his Studland retreat. (He owned a property in Studland from around 1897 to 1911. A bevy of Edwardian beauties watches the dramatic scene.

'HAVING A LOVELY TIME, WISH YOU WERE HERE.' This postcard was sent on 30 August 1912 and typifies the carefree innocence of youth. Two years later Britain would be at war.

'JUST FOR FUN', July 1902.

'ALL ABOARD FOR THE *EMPRESS*', July 1902. Lulworth Cove was a regular run for the paddle steamers *Empress* and *Victoria*, both of which had specially strengthened bows so they could 'beach' to allow passengers to board. The *Empress* was built in 1879 for Cosens and Co. In 1946 she appeared (suitably disguised) in David Lean's film version of Dickens' *Great Expectations*. She was scrapped in 1955, although her engines are preserved at the Maritime Museum in Southampton.

THE PADDLE STEAMER *PREMIER* leaving Swanage Bay, *c.* 1884. Another season over.


# ACKNOWLEDGEMENTS

We are most grateful to the following people for the loan of photographs and for providing information contained in this book:

Peter Ashton • Bill Bainbridge • Jack Baiss • Eric Bichard • Ivor Bragg Jack Chinchen • John Chinchen • Geoff Coffin • Tom Crook • John Dean Mrs Helen Dunman (née Muspratt) • Bob Dwen • Eric Gosney • Bryan Green Miss Keely Green • Arthur Hancock • Tom Hancock • Vic Harding Mrs Eileen Hardy • George Hardy • Lew Hardy • Murray Hardy • Ron Hardy Ray Harris • Keith Hastie • Neville Hibbs • Ray Hibbs • Jack Hixson Pete Hollins • Nigel Humphries • Mrs Linda Jackson • Ron Jackson Mrs Lisa Lambeth • Ted Langdon • David Lewer • Mrs M.J. Mason Dick Mayo • Eddie Noades • Julien Parker • Stephen Parker • Arthur Parsons Chris Phillips • Miss F.E. Phillips • the late Alex Powell • Purbeck Press Mrs Betty Purchase • Montague Purchase • Ken Redout • Pete Renaut Mike Rigglesworth • Fred Riley • Mrs Dorothy Rutherford • John Rutherford Jack Satherley • Daniel Smith • Mike Smith • Arthur Stanley • Swanage Fire Station • Tithe Barn Museum • Bill Tomes • Frank Tomes • Gordon Tomes Mrs Pam Vinton • Mrs Kay Webb • Kevin Wells • Mrs Nicky Wells.

Particular thanks are due to Sarah Jackson for typing the captions and deciphering our handwriting.


The accuracy of the facts in this book have been checked as carefully as possible. However, original sources can contain errors and memories fade. Please contact the authors if you have any further information or would be prepared to lend original photographs for copying, and possible display at the Tithe Barn Museum.